THE OFFICIAL
HIBERNIAN
ANNUAL 2022

Written by David Forsyth
Designed by Patryk Przewoźny

A Grange Publication

ISBN 978-1-913578-75-6

CONTENTS

Welcome

Welcome to the latest edition of the official Hibernian FC Annual – back after an enforced year off due to the coronavirus pandemic!

As we always do, we take a look back at the season that has passed and ahead to the future. And what a year we have seen, with Covid-19 wreaking havoc with our lives and with football, inevitably, caught up in the battle to bring the virus under control.

A season cut short, followed by a season played behind closed doors has been unparalleled in our game's history. But thanks to the efforts of everyone at the club and most importantly the incredible backing of you, our fantastic supporters, we came through in good order.

In particular we enjoyed a successful 2020-21 season on the pitch, with Jack Ross leading the players to a third-placed finish in Scotland's top flight for the first time in 16 years, earning a welcome return to European competition in the process. The team also managed to win through to the final of the Scottish Cup and the semi-final of the League Cup. Unfortunately, those prizes eluded us in those final stages but a third-place league finish, a final and a semi-final have created a fantastic base to build from!

Off the pitch, there has been a lot to talk about too, with the arrival of our new Chief Executive and with the unveiling of the Club's exciting strategic vision and plan to see Hibernian enjoy sustainable success on and off the pitch. We want to make our fans and our city proud, to create the most exciting matchday experience in Scotland, and to make our stadium the envy of the country.

Meantime, enjoy the Annual with its features on our playing stars, its look behind the scenes, and its quizzes and fun pages.

SEASON REVIEW

From the start, the 2020-21 campaign was to be a season like no other. Kicking off with all games behind closed doors with the hope – dashed as the season progressed – that we would see fans back inside Easter Road during the campaign.

Despite the uncertainty, Hibernian fans stepped up to back their club in droves with 11,000 buying season tickets understanding that they might have to watch games live only through the new livestreaming arrangements.

August

Competitive fixtures kicked off in August with a 2-1 home win against Kilmarnock, with Martin Boyle striking twice in a superb first half showing from the Hibees. Chris Burke got Killie back into it just before the break, but Hibernian saw out the game to record their first three points. Next up was an away trip to Livingston, which the team negotiated in emphatic fashion scoring four through Doidge and a Nisbet hat-trick, answered only a Dykes penalty.

Another tricky away trip, to newly promoted Dundee United, was next up and the match was a tough, hard-fought affair separated only by a well-taken Christian Doidge strike. Three games down and maximum points gained saw Hibernian start the season well. Motherwell were next up, visiting Easter Road, in a match that ended all square and scoreless, and this was followed by a difficult away trip to meet St Johnstone in Perth which, happily, ended 0-1 in Hibernian's favour with Stevie Mallan scoring from the penalty spot.

The season had started brilliantly, with four wins and a draw in August, but the month was to end with a first defeat. A 1-0 loss at Easter Road to Aberdeen was harsh on the men in green and white as chances were spurned before Ferguson scored from a penalty early in the second half.

September

September was to be a quieter month, with three fixtures being played.

First up was a trip to Paisley to meet a good St Mirren side, though the Buddies were struggling to find early season form. Goals from Nisbet, Newell and Boyle saw Hibernian win 0-3 in a match that was tighter than the scoreline suggested.

A first encounter with the Old Firm was next on the agenda, with Rangers and Celtic to be faced in quick succession.

Rangers came to visit Easter Road after a flying start. In a thrilling match Hibs took the lead through a Drey Wright goal before strikes from Morelos and Arfield either side of half-time saw the lead switch to Rangers. However, a goal from Christian Doidge levelled the match and ensured Hibernian gained a deserved share of the points. Next up was a visit to Parkhead to visit Celtic, who were in imperious form in one of their best performances of their season to rout Hibs 3-0.

October

October was to bring another flurry of matches in a condensed season, with League Cup ties plus the Scottish Cup semi-final v Hearts postponed from season 2019/20 to be played at Hampden alongside league fixtures.

The month kicked off well enough. A home encounter with Hamilton Accies was going well, with Hibs taking a three goal lead through a Nisbet double and Hanlon. However, a late rally from the Accies saw them strike twice to produce a nervy finish, with Hibs making it over the winning line.

League Cup fixtures were next up, with Hibs winning 3-1 at home to Brora Rangers through two goals from Mallan and one from Hanlon; a 1-2 win on the road to Cove Rangers with goals from Nisbet and Gullan; and a 0-1 win away at Forfar thanks to a David Gray goal.

League business recommenced with a 0-0 draw away with Ross County, with chances frustratingly missed to complete the first round of league fixtures. A trip to Kilmarnock was next, and again Hibernian came out on top – this time 0-1 thanks to a Nisbet penalty.

The month was to end with one of the season's big disappointments. A trip to Hampden to finally play the postponed 2019-20 Scottish Cup semi-final against arch-rivals Hearts saw Hibernian dominate large parts of the game, fail to take their chances, and eventually lose to an extra-time penalty.

November

November was another busy month, with Pittodrie the first port of all for Jack Ross' side. A slow start saw Hibernian go 2-0 down to the Dons, and while the team worked back into the game no further goals meant the points stayed up north. League Cup business was next up, with Dundee visitors to Easter Road in a final group match. A return to strong form saw Mallan strike to give Hibs the lead before Dundee levelled in the 71st minute, however late goals from Nisbet, Gullan and Hallberg ensured that Hibs were worthy winners. Two draws were to follow, a 2-2 affair against Celtic at Easter Road that saw second half strikes from Murphy and Nisbet cancelled out by two late strikes from Celtic, the second coming in injury time. Next St Johnstone came calling, and this time Hibernian had to battle back twice to level the game 2-2, with a rare brace from 'Mr Consistency', Paul McGinn. By one of those strange quirks of fate, Hibernian drew Dundee at Easter Road again in the League Cup, this time emerging winners by virtue of a Murphy goal.

December

December – with seven games to cram in - kicked off in great style. A 0-3 away win against Motherwell, with goals from Boyle, Doidge and McGinn was followed up with the biggest away win of the season, a 0-4 beating of Hamilton Academicals with Boyle, Doidge, McGinn

and Nisbet all on the scoresheet.

A quarter-final away to Alloa in the League Cup was up next, with Hibs winning the tie 1-2 after going in at the break a goal down. Second-half strikes from Doidge were enough to see the Hibees through to a semi-final tie with St Johnstone.

The return of league business saw Hibernian lose an injury time goal to Dundee United at Easter Road to concede a lead gained through the boot of Kyle Magennis for a disappointing draw. A Nisbet goal the following week saw Hibernian beat St Mirren 1-0 at home to gain another three points. In the two final fixtures, Rangers emerged victorious at Easter Road by virtue of a solitary goal in a hard-fought contest, but the month was to end with a disappointing away loss to Ross County at Easter Road, with the visitors under the guidance of former Hibee John Hughes winning 0-2.

January

The New Year continued with Hibernian's brief blip in form continuing, the team going down 0-3 at Easter Road to a resurgent Livingston, before the team returned to Parkhead to face Celtic. The game proved to be a thriller, with the spoils shared in a 1-1 draw with an injury time Nisbet goal earning the Hibees a well-earned point.

The visit of a Kilmarnock side struggling in the league saw Hibernian back to winning ways with goals from a Gogic wonder strike and an OG earning a 2-0 victory. A difficult trip to Hampden was next in the League Cup semi-final, with St Johnstone showing great form after a slow start to the season. A 3-0 loss meant a disappointed Hibs returned to Edinburgh empty handed, and things were no easier in the league when the team visited Ibrox to play high-flying Rangers. Despite a terrific showing, Hibs were unlucky to lose out 1-0 to a Morelos goal.

The month was to end in more optimistic fashion. An away trip to Tannadice saw the team hit their stride again, with a 0-2 away win earned by a rare McGregor goal and one from Boyle.

February

February's league card was to see Hibernian gain nine points from a possible 12. The month started with three successive wins. An away trip to Paisley saw St Mirren beaten 1-2, with goals from Porteous and a Boyle penalty. The following fixture saw the team deliver one of their most convincing performances of the season when they saw off close rivals Aberdeen 2-0 at Easter Road, a scoreline that flattered the Dons.

Boyle again struck from the penalty spot, and followed up with his second of the game, one goal coming in each half in a thoroughly high-level, attacking performance.

The visit of Brian Rice's Hamilton saw Hibernian pick up another three points, with goals from Boyle and Doig earning a 2-0 win, before the month ended with a sole defeat. A home loss to Motherwell brought a disappointing end to what had been an excellent month.

March

St Johnstone in Perth lay in wait next. The Saints excellent form was continuing, and

a goal from Craig was enough to see them keep the three points at home. A trip to Dingwall provided an opportunity to get back on track, and to avenge an earlier 0-2 home defeat to the Highland side, and goals from Boyle (from the penalty spot) and Doidge saw the Hibs win 1-2.

The month was to end in Livingston, where a 1-1 hard-fought draw on the artificial surface was earned through a Doidge equaliser.

April

April was to spring a busy schedule, with a run of Scottish Cup ties as well as two league fixtures were to be played.

The month kicked off in Dumfries, with a tricky away tie against Queen of the South, however goals from Boyle and a Doidge double seeing Hibs win 1-3 and progress to the next round.

Rangers at Ibrox in the league saw another end-to-end match, with the Glasgow side edging a 2-1 thriller with the Hibernian goal being scored by Nisbet.

Another away Cup tie, this time at Stranraer, saw Jack Ross' team progress thanks to a comfortable 0-4 win with the goals scored by Doidge, Nisbet and a Boyle double.

The league action continued at Livingston, with goals from Nisbet and Doyle putting Hibs firmly in control. A strike late in the game saw Livingston lose 1-2 and Hibs net all three points.

April ended with a Scottish Cup quarter-final tie, at home to Motherwell. Hibernian appeared to be in cruise control, opening up a two-goal lead through second-half strikes by Doidge and Irvine. However late pressure mounted by Motherwell saw two late goals conceded to take the tie into extra time, which failed to separate the teams. Hibernian held their nerve to win the tie on penalties. Another Cup semi-final at Hampden beckoned.

May

The month opened with a home loss to St Johnstone, who were proving Hibs' bogey team, with a 0-1 loss.

A Scottish Cup semi-final trip to Hampden to face Dundee United saw the Hibees looking to make another final, the first since the epic win of May 2016. The game saw the team back on track, winning 0-2 with goals from Nisbet in the first half and Doidge after the break earning the place in the final and ending the semi-final hoodoo.

A trip to Pittodrie to face Aberdeen saw Hibs record another win over the Dons - a Doidge goal separating the sides and lengthening the points gap between third and fourth in the league. The final league match of the season saw Celtic visit Easter Road, and a nil-nil draw saw Hibernian's league campaign end with a rewarding third-place finish for the first time in 16 years.

Only the Scottish Cup final remained, against St Johnstone, who had upset Hibernian in both the League and League Cup already.

Sadly, their strong form against Hibernian continued in the season's showpiece. Hibernian had gone into the game determined to repeat the cup-winning exploits of 2016, but it was Saints who emerged winners by the solitary goal of the game. The Saints had earned a remarkable Cup double after earlier defeating Livingston in the League Cup final.

Hibernian's season was over – but with a third-place finish, a Cup final and a League Cup semi-final the team had shown much to be excited about and build upon.

2020-21 SEASON QUIZ

1. How many semi-final appearances did Hibernian make during the season?

2. What was the Club's biggest winning margin in a league fixture during the season?

3. Which former Hibs cup winner made his final appearance for Celtic against Hibs in May 2021?

4. What league position did Hibernian achieve for the first time in 16 years?

5. Which team did Hibernian play in the first league fixture?

6. Which former Hibs star and Hibs TV expert pundit was appointed to manage Ross County during the season?

7. Which Hibs star scored the Hibernian Goal of the Season?

8. Name the Hibernian star who went on loan to Inverness Caledonian Thistle after recuperating from illness?

9. Who did Hibernian defeat in the semi-final of the 2020-21 Scottish Cup?

10. What was the club's "first in UK" front of shirt sponsorship in season 2020-21?

11. Who did Hibernian play in the Scottish Cup Final?

12. Name the goalkeeping coach who joined Hibernian in the 2020 close season?

13. From which team was Kyle Magennis signed in October 2020?

14. Martin Boyle was one of two Socceroo Aussie internationals who played at Hibs in season 2020-21. Name the other?

NEW RECRUITS

Jake Doyle-Hayes

Irishman Jake Doyle-Hayes joined Hibernian on a two-year deal in June 2021.

The midfielder was a regular presence in a strong St Mirren side last season, making 30 appearances for the Buddies. As well as achieving their highest league placing in years, St Mirren also competed in two cup semi-finals.

An Under-21 cap for the Republic of Ireland, he started his career at Aston Villa. He has also turned out at Cheltenham Town and Cambridge United. Hibernian saw off competition for Jake's signature.

The versatile midfielder can play as a holding player, but also enjoys a more dynamic box-to-box role and is hoping his move to Hibs can see him score more regularly, after netting once for The Saints.

On signing at Easter Road he said: "Coming into a squad where we are looking to challenge for medals is something I want to be a part of. Looking at the players there are some unbelievable talents and I'm looking forward to being a part of that."

Daniel Mackay

20-year-old Daniel was a man in demand after impressing at Inverness Caledonian Thistle under bosses John Robertson and Neil McCann.

Goal-scoring midfielder Daniel had caught the eye after notching up both the Players Young Player of the Year and Supporters Young Player of the Year awards at the Highland club.

While several clubs were chasing his services, it was Hibernian who won out thanks, Daniel said, to the impression Head Coach Jack Ross made allied with the positive way in which his family were treated by the Easter Road staff.

The fee paid for Daniel represents the Club's continued ambition to be the best club in Scotland for talented young players.

Sporting Director Graeme Mathie said at the signing: "In all the conversations we have had with Daniel, his family and his representatives, it was clear that they all see Hibernian as the right place to continue to develop his career."

"Sir" David Gray

Hardly a new recruit, but a new role for one of the most familiar faces to perform at Easter Road in many years.

David Gray, cup-winning skipper and club legend, decided to hang up his boots and call time on his illustrious playing career and join the coaching staff at Hibernian.

David, who nodded home the winning goal at 90+2 minutes to bring the cup to Easter Road that May day in 2016, is now first-team coach.

Head Coach Jack Ross was delighted to welcome David to the coaching staff and said: "He has demonstrated brilliant leadership qualities and a desire to learn about the game from a tactical and man management perspective."

David decided that it was time to take the next step in his career after the "absolute privilege and honour" of playing for and captaining Hibernian. Supporters would say the admiration is entirely mutual.

MARTIN BOYLE

It's not too often you sign a potential World Cup star who spent much of his formative football life in Montrose – but a happy story continued to run at Easter Road when star man Martin Boyle extended his contract with the Club till 2024.

The flying winger - who has been starring for Australia's Socceroos as they aim for the World Cup in Qatar in 2022 - delighted Head Coach Jack Ross, team-mates and supporters when he put pen-to-paper this summer on a new deal in the face of interest from other clubs.

Boyler cuts a contented figure in Easter Road, happy in the knowledge that his own ambitions are aligned with those of a Club determined to build a sustainable, successful future. He signed from Dundee in 2015 after starting out at Montrose.

And with a wife, Rachael, who is also

starring in the famous green and white for Hibernian Women, we can only hope that Martin remains a fixture at Easter Road for some time to come.

Martin enjoyed his best-ever season last season, with 15 goals in all competitions and 13 assists. On his decision, he said: "Everyone can see how much I am enjoying myself here. It is great to be at a club that means so much to me and my family."

Boyler's career path began in the east of Scotland and has been far from easy or straightforward. He said: "Everyone has different career paths. It was great playing for Montrose. I was 16 or 17 years old going into a big boy dressing room and that was an eye-opener.

"I got work through an agency, where

to do when I was a little boy was be a professional footballer and thankfully I have done that."

A member of the 2016 Scottish Cup winning squad, Martin has signed with a keen eye on the future.

"As a team we're always looking to improve and that's key for me. Everyone can see the desire from the club, the players, and the management staff to progress and challenge for trophies and European football; that excites me and that's where I want to be.

"If we keep working hard, then hopefully we will be able to create more highs."

every week I did something different. I helped build Donald Trump's golf course, doing all the sand dunes and digging out the weeds and all that. So, thanks to him.

"Then I would be unloading boxes off the back of a lorry and putting them into vans. I was doing a lot of stuff like that. Every week was different. It was mayhem then I left work to go to training at night but I had young legs so I could run round them all. It was great.

"So I know I'm in a privileged position now where I come into my work every day with a smile on my face. All I wanted

Hibernian Community Foundation

Who Are Hibernian Community Foundation?

As the official charity of Hibernian Football Club, we are fortunate to be able to use the unique appeal of Hibernian to reach out and improve lives. We are proud to have our home within the South Stand at Easter Road Stadium.

What we do:

We're proud of the difference we have made to people's lives since our creation in 2008 and we are proud that Hibernian Football Club through Hibernian Community Foundation is changing lives for the better.

We are passionate about working closer with our communities and creating opportunities for people to lead healthier lives, improving education and employment opportunities, and being good citizens for and of Edinburgh and the Lothians.

We will work with communities across Edinburgh and the Lothians with a particular focus on:

- Children, young people, adults and families
- Disadvantaged communities
- Disadvantaged people

More Than Football:

Hibernian Community Foundation are proud to be more than football as we use the attraction point of Hibernian Football club to positively impact health, education, social inclusion and the environment.

Hibs owner Ron Gordon: "As a club – and in partnership with our Foundation – we want to connect, motivate, inspire and help people within our communities. We aspire to be more than a football club and help the vulnerable and disadvantaged..

Community Foundation Projects

The Greenest Club: Football provides a global platform to promote sustainable and responsible energy and resource consumption. Hibernian Community Foundation strive to ensure that all future interventions and activities will have a neutral or very low impact on the health of the planet.

The Foundation and Hibernian Football Club are working together to make Edinburgh and the Lothians Green. So far, Hibernian Community Foundation have recycled over 2.5 tonnes of food that would otherwise go to waste. Clothes, toys and school resources have also been recycled within Foundation projects.

The Famous Five A Day:

Hibernian Community Foundation work with local partner schools in Edinburgh and East Lothian to provide weekend food parcels to families. This project was launched in May 2020 and has seen the Foundation deliver over 60,000 food items out so far. It is important for us all to lead a healthy life, this starts by eating good quality food.

Football Opportunities:

Hibernian Community Foundation have opportunities for young players to wear the famous green and white strip through representing the Community Foundation Squads. Academy players develop technical,

tactical, physical, psychological and social skills.

- Boys Community Football Teams players born between 2010 and 2015
- Girls Community Football Teams players born between 2003 and 2015

Award Winning Hibernian Community Foundation

- Scottish Football Association's Best Professional Club in the Community - 2018
- Scottish Football Association's South East Region's Best Project – Hibs Class 2020

How to contact Hibernian Community Foundation

Email:
info@hiberniancommunityfoundation.org.uk

Website:
www.hiberniancommunityfoundation.org.uk

Twitter:
@hibsincommunity

Facebook:
Hibernian

Community Foundation Instagram:
@Hibernian

Community Foundation LinkedIn:
Hibernian Community Foundation Limited

SQUAD PROFILES

Josh
Doig

Josh Doig is rightly regarded as one of the brightest emerging talents in Scottish football. The rampaging left-back was named Scottish Football Writers' Association Young Player of the Year after a stunning breakthrough campaign. His progress was reflected in a new four-year contract and a first Scotland Under-21 call-up but the down-to-earth prospect still knocks on Head Coach Jack Ross' door to check he's okay to head home from Hibernian Training Centre (HTC) after training.

Paul
Hanlon

Paul Hanlon, as the song goes, is a Hibee through and through.

A boyhood supporter of the club and a product of a fruitful Academy system, Hanlon has lived the dream at the heart of our defence for more than a decade now.

There was no prouder man when he lifted the Scottish Cup in 2016 but he's showing no signs of slowing down, with a first Scotland cap last term before he was formally named David Gray's successor as captain in the summer.

Ryan Porteous

Ryan Porteous is another who has made the step from the terraces to the first team.

The Academy graduate and former Scotland Under-21 captain is now an established performer, with a number of statistics able to underline his promise as a dominant, ball-playing centre-back.

Mentored by sporting icon – and Hibernian supporter – Andy Murray, Ryan is well on the way to emulating the Easter Road heroes he once looked up to.

Lewis Stevenson

What more can be said about Lewis Stevenson? At this stage he surely needs no introduction.

The modern-day club legend is the only player in the history of the club to have won both the League Cup and Scottish Cup during his spell with The Hibees.

The admiration for his consistency on the park is matched by his charitable deeds off it, with The Hanlon Stevenson Foundation – set up alongside team-mate Paul Hanlon – proudly supporting several local causes in Edinburgh.

Darren McGregor

Darren McGregor was born to wear the Hibernian shirt and plays every game as if it's his last.

Darren's dream move to Easter Road didn't come until later on in his career but he's certainly made up for lost time and is one of the Scottish Cup-winning immortals.

His influence extends far beyond the pitch and we have to hope he'll continue to help shape the club for years to come.

Sean Mackie

Between trying to dislodge long-serving left-back Lewis Stevenson and his own injury problems, Sean Mackie hasn't had the easiest time of it.

However, the Academy graduate sees the setbacks as character building and is keen to remind people why he was so highly thought of when he made his top-team breakthrough.

Powerful and blessed with a clean strike of the ball.

Kyle Magennis

Kyle Magennis is starting to show exactly why Hibernian handed him a five-year contract when he was snapped up from St Mirren.

Magennis had to be patient when he initially arrived at Easter Road, as he worked his way back to full fitness following a long-term lay-off, but Jack Ross never doubted the potential of the all-action midfielder.

The former Buddies captain and Scotland Under-21 international adds drive and physicality to the midfield and is one to watch this season.

Drey Wright

Drey Wright was once described by former St Johnstone boss Tommy Wright as the most talented player he'd ever worked with.

A hard-working, tricky winger, Drey came through the ranks at Colchester United but really caught the eye during two seasons at McDiarmid Park.

His first goal in the green and white came in a pulsating 2-2 draw with Rangers in September 2020.

Joe Newell

Joe Newell, by his own admission, took time to find his feet at Hibernian but the midfielder has certainly made up for lost time.

Joe possesses the kind of class that Hibs fans love – able to glide forward effortlessly with the ball at his feet, with menacing deliveries from set-pieces.

Joe's laid-back demeanour disguises a fierce competitor, who gave everyone at Easter Road a boost when he elected to sign a new contract and turn his back on interest from England.

Alex Gogic

Alex Gogic is a gentleman off the pitch and a warrior on it. The former Hamilton midfielder – who has earned full international honours with Cyprus during his time at Easter Road – played a big part in The Hibees' being able to boast the third-best defensive record in last season's Premiership.

He hassles and harries so that others can flourish and quickly won the respect of his team-mates at HTC.

Melker Hallberg

Melker Hallberg is a man of few words who prefers to do his talking on the park.

The Swede, who is a full international, made his first-team debut at the tender age of 13.

An unselfish player who can operate in a number of roles, he's also a threat from set-pieces.

Scott Allan

Scott Allan is adored by the Hibernian support, who could watch re-runs of his through-balls all day.

A born entertainer who possesses that rare gift of being able to spot, and then play, passes other people don't even see, Scott's now in his third spell at Easter Road.

He's found a home and football fulfilment in Leith and is an ambassador for Diabetes UK in his spare time.

Chris Cadden

Chris Cadden is a man on a mission to add to his two full Scotland caps and that can only be a good thing for Hibernian.

The former Motherwell man has had an injury-disrupted start to life at the club, but his potential is unmistakable.

The only issue is tying him down to one position, such is his comfort in playing at right-back, right wing-back or across the midfield.

Steven Bradley

Steven Bradley is an exciting winger looking to make a name for himself.

He joined from Queen's Park in the summer of 2019 and quickly made an impression on the staff at HTC.

Jack Ross has patiently eased him into the first-team set-up and spoken on more than one occasion about the belief he has in Bradley to make the grade.

Josh Campbell

Josh Campbell has worked his way back to the first-team squad after an impressive loan spell with Edinburgh City.

The combative midfielder and Academy graduate previously enjoyed a taste of the action in the League Cup under Paul Heckingbottom and is hungry for more.

He can be pleased with his appearance in our head-to-head with Andorrans Santa Coloma in July.

Martin Boyle

He's the star man, playing on the right. His name is Martin Boyle and he's, well, dynamite.

A larger than life personality shouldn't detract from total commitment to his craft, with Boyle having improved year-on-year to become one of the most potent attacking threats in Scottish football and an established Australian international.

He's terrorised many a full-back but is arguably not even the best player in his own household, given his wife is Hibernian Women star Rachael.

Daniel MacKay

Hibernian were quick to secure the pre-contract signing of in-demand winger Daniel MacKay, in the face of rival interest from north and south of the border.

MacKay was able to train with his new team-mates after the completion of his season with Inverness Caledonian Thistle, which helped give him a head start on the new campaign.

Recently capped by Scotland's Under-21s for the first time, he's sure to excite Easter Road supporters with his direct, tricky style of play.

Jamie Murphy

Jamie Murphy added real class and experience to the group, having come a long way from the boy who broke through the ranks with such style at Motherwell and quickly became their all-time top scorer in European competition.

Successful stints with Sheffield United, Brighton, Rangers and Burton Albion helped develop his all-round game.

Whether he's hugging the touchline or drifting inside opponents, there aren't many better sights in Scottish football than Murphy in full flow.

Kevin Nisbet

Kevin Nisbet is a star on the rise and one of the feel-good stories of recent years in Scottish football.

Nisbet's earned his stripes the hard way, after a difficult spell at Partick Thistle was followed by three fruitless loan spells. He found his feet at Raith Rovers, the goals continued to flow at Dunfermline and he never looked back. The turnaround was capped by a call-up to the Scotland squad for the Euros – inspired by a thoroughly impressive first season at Hibernian.

Christian Doidge

A firm favourite with team-mates and supporters alike, Christian Doidge, is the type to lead from the front.

His selfless shifts never go unnoticed, while his prolific form in front of goal has marked him out as one of the leading strikers in Scottish football.

Left bed-ridden by a case of COVID-19 in the summer of 2021 he's had to play catch-up to work his way to full match fitness but, even in early cameos from the bench, his influence on the team is never in doubt.

Jamie Gullan

You'll struggle to find anyone at HTC with a bad word to say about Jamie Gullan, such is the appreciation of his determination and work ethic – coupled with a lethal strike of the ball that earned him his 'Hammer' nickname.

He's equally popular at Raith Rovers, having enjoyed three productive loan spells in Kirkcaldy.

First-team opportunities have been hard to come by, given the form of those ahead of him in the pecking order, but you can be sure he's ready to make the most of any chance that comes his way.

PLAYER QUIZ

1. Which Hibernian player appeared for Scotland during the UEFA Euro 2020?

2. Who joined Hibernian in January 2021 from Columbus Crew in the USA?

3. Which Cypriot international plays for Hibs?

4. Who finished as the club's leading goalscorer?

5. Which player appeared in every league fixture in 2020-21?

6. Who was named the Scottish Football Writers Young Player in 2021?

7. Which player was named the Hibernian Players Player in 2021?

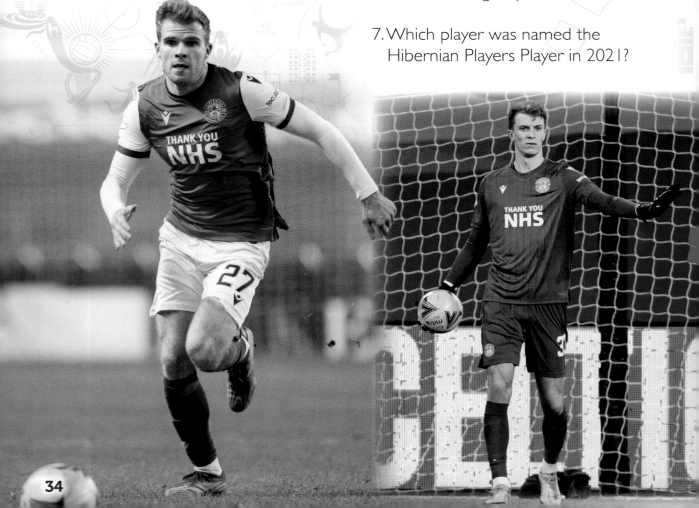

HIBS KIDS

Season 2021/2022 Planner

Home Game

Away Game

Hibs Kids Game

Post-Split Matches

	vs		
Saturday, Apr 23 2022	RESULT		v
Saturday, Apr 30 2022	RESULT		v
Saturday, May 7 2022	RESULT		v
Wednesday, May 11 2022	RESULT		v
Saturday, May 14 2022	RESULT		v

Motherwell vs **HIBERNIAN**
Sunday, Aug 1 2021
RESULT ☐ v ☐

HIBERNIAN vs Ross County
Saturday, Aug 7 2021
RESULT ☐ v ☐

Dundee vs **HIBERNIAN**
Saturday, Aug 21 2021
RESULT ☐ v ☐

HIBERNIAN vs Livingston
Saturday, Aug 28 2021
RESULT ☐ v ☐

Hearts vs **HIBERNIAN**
Saturday, Sept 11 2021
RESULT ☐ v ☐

HIBERNIAN vs St Mirren
Saturday, Sept 18 2021
RESULT ☐ v ☐

HIBERNIAN vs St Johnstone
Saturday, Sept 25 2021
RESULT ☐ v ☐

Rangers vs **HIBERNIAN**
Saturday, Oct 2 2021
RESULT ☐ v ☐

HIBERNIAN vs Dundee Utd
Saturday, Oct 16 2021
RESULT ☐ v ☐

Aberdeen vs **HIBERNIAN**
Saturday, Oct 23 2021
RESULT ☐ v ☐

HIBERNIAN vs Celtic
Wednesday, Oct 27 2021
RESULT ☐ v ☐

Ross County vs **HIBERNIAN**
Saturday, Oct 30 2021
RESULT ☐ v ☐

Livingston vs **HIBERNIAN**
Saturday, Nov 6 2021
RESULT ☐ v ☐

HIBERNIAN vs Dundee
Saturday, Nov 20 2021
RESULT ☐ v ☐

St Johnstone vs **HIBERNIAN**
Saturday, Nov 27 2021
RESULT ☐ v ☐

HIBERNIAN vs Rangers
Wednesday, Dec 1 2021
RESULT ☐ v ☐

HIBERNIAN vs Motherwell
Saturday, Dec 4 2021
RESULT ☐ v ☐

St Mirren vs **HIBERNIAN**
Saturday, Dec 11 2021
RESULT ☐ v ☐

HIBERNIAN vs Aberdeen
Saturday, Dec 18 2021
RESULT ☐ v ☐

Dundee Utd vs **HIBERNIAN**
Sunday, Dec 26 2021
RESULT ☐ v ☐

Celtic vs **HIBERNIAN**
Wednesday, Dec 29 2021
RESULT ☐ v ☐

HIBERNIAN vs Hearts
Sunday, Jan 2 2022
RESULT ☐ v ☐

Motherwell vs **HIBERNIAN**
Wednesday, Jan 26 2022
RESULT ☐ v ☐

HIBERNIAN vs Livingston
Saturday, Jan 29 2022
RESULT ☐ v ☐

HIBERNIAN vs St Mirren
Saturday, Feb 5 2022
RESULT ☐ v ☐

Rangers vs **HIBERNIAN**
Wednesday, Feb 9 2022
RESULT ☐ v ☐

HIBERNIAN vs Ross County
Saturday, Feb 19 2022
RESULT ☐ v ☐

HIBERNIAN vs Celtic
Saturday, Feb 26 2022
RESULT ☐ v ☐

Dundee vs **HIBERNIAN**
Wednesday, Mar 2 2022
RESULT ☐ v ☐

HIBERNIAN vs St Johnstone
Saturday, Mar 5 2022
RESULT ☐ v ☐

Aberdeen vs **HIBERNIAN**
Saturday, Mar 19 2022
RESULT ☐ v ☐

HIBERNIAN vs Dundee Uutd
Saturday, Apr 2 2022
RESULT ☐ v ☐

Hearts vs **HIBERNIAN**
Saturday, Apr 9 2022
RESULT ☐ v ☐

HIBERNIAN WOMEN

While Hibernian Women brought in a number of new faces to their squad over the summer, there was a heightened sense of intrigue and anticipation surrounding the arrival of three players in particular.

Head Coach Dean Gibson had set his sights on America and was able to secure

the services of three talented American players in Gabby English, Toni Malone and Alexa Coyle. The trio have been able to provide depth and quality all over the pitch – English is a goalkeeper, Malone can play anywhere across the midfield and provide cover at left-back, and Coyle is adept as a striker or a winger.

English has had experience of European football in the past – the 24-year-old plied her trade in Portugal for a time, turning out for Boavista in Porto before making the move back State-side to join Orlando Pride in her native Florida. The deal to bring English to Scotland was agreed back in February while the SWPL season was suspended, and she would make her first appearance in Hibs' opening SWPL Cup match against Kilmarnock, keeping a clean sheet in a 4-0 win.

Also playing a part in that match was Coyle, who opened her Hibs account by scoring the opening goal of the match by way of a penalty, which she had won. Unlike her fellow Americans, Coyle is experiencing European football for the first time, having joined the club from the University of Montana, spending four years with the Grizzlies, scoring five goals in 11 games in her senior year. Not the only athlete in her family, Coyle's brother Brock

We asked Head Coach of Hibernian Women, Dean Gibson, for his thoughts on his new American stars – he had this to say:

"When these players became available it was a no-brainer to try and convince them to join Hibernian. Thankfully, after various chats, they all agreed it was the next stage of their journey.

"I think they have settled in really well. The players are very receptive to information, so it's not taken long for them to get to grips with what we want.

is a former football player – American football, mind you!

The only member of Hibs' American contingent to miss out on the season opener against Kilmarnock was Malone, whose arrival to the capital was delayed until the same weekend. Malone has also had experience of European football, having spent a year at FC Wacker Innsbruck in the OFB Frauen Bundesliga, but having suffered an ankle injury midway through the season, Malone spent much of her time in Austria watching from the sidelines. She's raring to make up for lost time and fight hard to secure Champions League football for the Hibees!

"We have signed players who are a good age and have played at a very good standard. They know what it takes to win, and that's exactly what we demand at Hibernian."

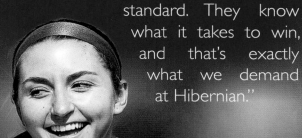

HIBERNIAN RIDDLER NICKNAME QUIZ

Answer the questions to come up with the nickname of a well known Hibee, past or present

1. A small Australian parakeet
2. One who fights as part of a Scottish Army
3. A closed vessel in which water is heated
4. A City in Northwest Portugal
5. Hollywood Romantic Comedy starring John Wayne, set in Ireland
6. Bulb vegetable of the species Allium
7. The Creator, Supreme Being – certainly in France
8. A diminutive individual with magical powers
9. He's smarter than the average bear
10. Rolled ground beef, often served with pasta
11. A single masted sailboat, typically with one headsail
12. A boxing legend – at least in tinseltown
13. One who rises in opposition
14. Famous honeycomb chocolate bar
15. An angry green giant – bit of a Marvel
16. Ballet giant or horseracing legend – take your pick

HAND IN GLOVES

You need a big personality to succeed in the high-profile world of goalkeeping in professional football – where every mistake gets noticed and very few go unpunished.

At Hibernian, we really do have guys who fill that role – in terms of physically and mentally!

Matt Macey stands an impressive 6ft 7ins tall, with number two keeper Kevin Dąbrowski not a lot shorter at close to 6ft 6ins. Big guys, with big hearts.

Matt joined Hibernian on loan in January this year, before signing a two-year contract at Easter Road in May. Head Coach said he had made "a brilliant impression" on everyone at the Club since his arrival and had been "terrific in the matches he's played."

The player signed from Premier League giants Arsenal, where he had spent several years of his career, playing twice for the first team in the EFL Cup and the UEFA Europa League. He also enjoyed loan spells at Accrington Stanley, Luton Town and Plymouth Argyle. He was a part of the matchday squad which won the FA Cup Final in 2020 against Chelsea.

Prior to signing for Arsenal – who beat off competition from Everton to land him – he had come through the youth system at Bristol Rovers.

The big goalie has taken over in goals at Hibernian from Israeli international Ofir Marciano, who left the club at the end of last season after a successful spell.

Matt said: "I'm enjoying it and I'm really happy here. Everyone around the club made me feel comfortable and within two or three days I had settled in and I think I've kicked on since."

Larger than life character Kevin Dąbrowski joined the Hibernian development squad from the youth side at Polish cracks Lech Poznań back in 2017.

The 23-year-old suffered a serious injury in training soon after he arrived that threatened to derail his career, but his

determination to overcome the setback impressed all at Hibernian Training Centre where he is renowned as a dedicated trainer. The affable Kevin (his real name is Maciej, by the way, he was "christened" Kevin by team-mates soon after arriving) is determined to become Hibernian's number one and will present Matt with real competition for the starting spot.

He has enjoyed productive loan spells which have helped him mature as a keeper, winning a standout Betfred cup tie against Hearts when he was at Cowdenbeath.

Kevin is loving his time at Hibernian. He says: "I'm very happy here, and I've been here for a few years now. I feel like it is my second home.

"I really enjoy working every day with Matt and the coaches, and it is simple for me. I want to become

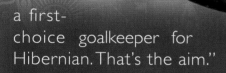

a first-choice goalkeeper for Hibernian. That's the aim."

At the start of the 2021/22 season, Kevin played the second-half in a pre-season friendly win against Matt's old club, Arsenal.

After making a brilliant free-kick stop, he stretched to stop a Pepe penalty – earning well-earned plaudits.

With two big personalities working as team-mates but still competing for the gloves, Hibernian's goalkeeping position is definitely up for grabs.

SPOT THE BALL

Can you spot the ball position in the match below?

EAT LIKE A HIBEE!

Our players work hard all week to be in the best possible condition for a matchday, and it's not just about what they do on the training pitch. Paola Rodriguez Giustiniani is our Performance Nutritionist. She makes sure the squad are eating and drinking all the right things to get them on top form.

What would the players' pre-match meal typically look like?

The pre-match meal is super important because it helps players top up their energy stores and this will delay fatigue during the game. The pre-match meal is usually consumed around three hours before kick-off. We serve a mix and match of breakfast and lunch foods. Players are advised to have plenty of carbohydrate (carbohydrates are the main source of energy for the muscles and the brain) options like breakfast cereals, pancakes, toast, rice, pasta, potatoes, sweet potatoes, fruits, among other carbohydrate-rich options along with a smaller portion of protein sources like scrambled eggs, chicken, salmon etc. We also encourage players to keep themselves hydrated before the game, so we make sure they ingest enough water and in some cases electrolyte and sports drinks.

Do they have any snacks just before the game or at half-time?

Yes, they do. We usually set up a nutrition station inside the dressing room. We offer carbohydrate-rich options that are easily digested like cereal bars, waffles, sports gels, sports gummies, bananas, grapes, confectionery (Wine Gums, Haribo, Jelly Babies), among other things. It is also important to remind them to hydrate, so we also provide them with sports drinks and water.

What kinds of things would they eat immediately afterwards?

Nutrition is very important for recovery so immediately after the match we offer players a recovery drink that will nurture and hydrate them at the same time. We usually offer recovery drinks that are especially formulated for recovery and also chocolate milk, which is a great option for recovery. After they have had this, we would usually offer them food. The food options will vary but they will usually get foods rich in protein and carbohydrates that are easy to grab like chicken wraps, burritos, pasta pots etc.

What's the strangest nutritional request you've ever had from a player?

I think it is important to understand that everything a football player does the game of the day will involve a little bit of routine and they usually want to keep their routine the same. Also, some players are very superstitious so that's another thing that as a nutritionist I have learned to respect. I would say that fat sources, even if they are the healthy ones, are not essential for match-performance but we have a player that needs to have an avocado on game-day no matter what. Nutritionally, an avocado is great, but it isn't essential for match-performance. However, this is very important for the player, so I make sure he gets his avocado on match-day. Apart from that we have some picky eaters in the squad, but nothing too serious.

You're also very sporty. What's your secret weapon in the kitchen?

I do love sports, especially running. I do pay attention to what I am eating, and I make it work depending on my goals. If I am preparing for a long-distance race, all my focus is on eating enough food to support my training and to avoid injuries. If I am just keeping myself fit or I am trying to improve my body composition, then I work a bit more on controlling food portions and getting exactly what I need, no more and no less. Then, on a general basis I consider super important to have a balanced diet that includes all the food groups, not to skip fruit and vegetable consumption, and to enjoy food, even the occasional treat, as food should be also an enjoyable experience.

PLAYER CHAT

We went behind-the-scenes at HTC and got the help of a secret footballer to spill the secrets on his team-mates. Can you guess who's who?

1. Our kitman is a secret Arsenal fan, so who has he been asking for a shirt to hang on the kit-room wall?

2. Which young defender has added Deacon Blue and Ronan Keating to the pre-match playlist? Ask your parents…

3. "A scrawny Welshman who is a terrible golfer." No prizes for guessing this one.

4. Name the midfielder who has a secret Pokémon tattoo.

5. Reckoned to be the strongest in the gym, who goes by the nickname 'Ginto'?

6. One of our strikers is described as 'the biggest moaner at the club'. Who do you think that is?

7. "He's like an eel, the way he jinks in and out with those hips. Do eels have hips?" . Who is our secret footballer describing?

8. Which player has been known to wear a Birmingham City strip on holiday? The team he supported as a kid.

9. Whose specialist subject in club quizzes is Europe's capital cities?

10. Name the player who dislocated his thumb three days into his trial at Hibs after being hit by a Jamie Gullan shot.

LOCAL HERO

Paul McGinn

It's probably fair to say that the signing of Paul McGinn from St Mirren in January 2020 was a fairly low-key affair…

But you'd be hard-pressed to find any Hibs fan who would now disagree with the statement that, pound for pound, his capture represents one of the shrewdest pieces of business the club has done in years.

Few if any players features more often on the matchday team-sheet than the dogged, determined and highly effective right back who has had to fill the big boots previously worn by David Gray. Paul has proven to be Hibernian's 'Mr Consistent', winning an international call-up in the process.

Paul didn't take much convincing to make the move east – after all younger brother "Super" John McGinn had made the same trip with some success! John was an integral part of the side that won the Scottish Cup under Alan Stubbs and clinched promotion back to the premiership with Neil Lennon before earning a big move to Aston Villa, for whom he now stars in the Premier League,

Head Coach Jack Ross, who had worked with Paul at St Mirren and before that at Dumbarton, described Paul as "a manager's dream. The type of player who is a good team-mate, first and foremost, and gives you everything he has on a weekly basis."

Paul, who was named as club vice-captain at the start of this season, penned a contract extension keeping him at Hibs till 2022 on the day he got his international call-up. He has spoken about the move to Hibs being "the break" he needed to move his game up a level.

He added of his determination to do well at Hibernian: "I'm at the age now where I've played a lot of games and can relax. It makes the game easier.

"We don't want to get carried away but our expectations are that we want to win, and if anyone else wants to win at Easter Road they will need to play really well.

"We want to be competing at the top end of the league and going deep into cup competitions, and winning silverware. That runs through the squad, from the gaffer down, and that is good to be part of."

Paul played all 38 league games last season, a tribute to his consistency and fitness levels. He also played in five Scottish Cup ties and four League Cup matches, a total of 47 appearances in which he scored three goals, including a memorable double.

Paul McGinn:

- Paul was born in Glasgow in October 1990
- Raised in Clydebank, he started his career as a youth player at Queen's Park
- He made his debut against Raith Rovers in 2009 when, after coming on as a substitute, he was sent off in the final minute
- His career has seen him also play at St Mirren, Dumbarton, Chesterfield, Dundee, and Partick Thistle

- Paul is one of three footballing brothers – with John and Stephen also enjoying spells with both St Mirren and Hibernian
- Grandad Jack is a former Chairman of Celtic and former President of the Scottish FA
- Paul is 175 cm tall (5ft 9ins)

10 FACTS ABOUT

Joe
Newell
CENTRAL-MIDFIELD

1 Joe was born in Tamworth, England, in March 1993

2 He came through youth football at Birmingham City

3 Joe made his competitive senior debut in 2011 for Peterborough United

4 He joined Championship side Rotherham United in 2015

5 He spent four years with Rotherham, which included a Wembley play-off fin al win

6 Joe signed for Hibs in summer of 2019

7 The midfielder signed an extended 2.5 year deal in 2021

8 Joe is around 6ft tall

9 Joe was controversially red-carded in a UEFA Conference League qualifier at Easter Road against Andorran opposition at the start of the 21/22 season – his first red card in six seasons

10 Post-match he tweeted to fans that he had enjoyed playing the game and jokingly signed himself #hatchetman

SPOT THE DIFFERENCE

There are 10 differences between these two photographs, can you spot them all?

LATE SIGNINGS

JAMES SCOTT

£1.5 million rated striker James Scott joined Hibernian on a season-long loan from Hull City FC in August.

James, capped at under 21 level for Scotland, joined the Tigers in a £1.5 million move from Motherwell in 2020, but injuries and illness hampered his progress at the Championship side.

"He is a young player with enormous potential and we believe we can help him achieve that," said Hibs head coach Jack Ross. "James is able to play anywhere across the front line and I am excited to both welcome him to the club and begin working with him."

For his part James was delighted to be joining the Easter Road side. He said: "I was very proud to make my debut for this club. I know it is the best place for me to be playing right now, and I want to show the Hibs fans what I can do."

DYLAN TAIT

Highly-rated Scottish youngster Dylan Tait signed for Hibernian from Raith Rovers for an undisclosed fee this summer and then,

as part of the transfer the 19-year-old was loaned back to the Fife side until January.

The deal for the midfielder will run until 2025, and the arrangement struck with Raith ensures Dylan can continue his development so he can hit the ground running in Jack Ross' first team.

"Dylan is someone that we identified last season as a young player with enormous potential," said Hibs Head Coach Jack Ross. "He continued to show his ability in Raith's early fixtures, and my staff and I are excited about working with him and continuing to develop his game."

Tait, who came through at Partick Thistle, made his professional debut for Raith Rovers in Scottish League 1, coming on as a substitute against Montrose aged just 18. During his breakthrough season, he helped the club win promotion to the Scottish Championship, scoring three goals and

setting up two in 23 league games. He also won their Young Player of the Year award. Dylan Tait said. "It's a massive club and I can't wait to get going.

"I've been playing for Raith Rovers in League 1 and the Championship, so this is obviously a massive step up for me, but I'm over the moon to get here."

DAVID MITCHELL

David Mitchell was signed from Clyde on August 31st to add competition to the goalkeeping department.

The experienced 31-year-old shot stopper put pen-to-paper on a deal which runs until 2023, and will work closely with goalkeeper coach Craig Samson as well as Matt Macey and Kevin Dabrowski.

Mitchell has made over 250 career appearances and has impressed of late with Scottish League One outfit, Clyde.

He's featured in the top three tiers of Scottish football and played for a plethora of clubs including Dundee and Falkirk.

NATHAN WOOD

England under 20 international Nathan Wood joined Hibernian on a season-long loan deal from Middlesbrough during the summer.

The highly-regarded young defender came through Boro's academy and became the club's youngest-ever player at the tender age of 16 years and 72 days. He came on as a substitute in the EFL Cup against Notts County in August 2018.

He continued to work with the first team and went on to make his league debut the following season.

Last year, he made seven appearances for the Championship side before joining League 1 club Crewe Alexandra in search for regular first team football; he made 12 appearances at Crewe and impressed in the heart of their backline.

After joining the club, Wood said: "I'm buzzing to be here, it's a big club, and I'm really excited to get going."

WORDSEARCH

Find the twelve Hibernian midfield generals from within this wordsearch

Russell LATAPY
Franck SAUZEE
Scott ALLAN
Merouane ZEMMAMA
Alex EDWARDS
Pat MCGINLAY
Bobby COMBE
John COLLINS
Des BREMNER
Kevin THOMSON
Pat STANTON
Guillaume BEUZELIN

Y	A	L	N	I	G	C	M	M	Z	N
Z	J	C	Y	S	T	A	N	T	O	N
N	X	C	P	Z	T	N	S	F	C	O
E	C	H	A	F	E	N	N	O	T	S
D	Z	F	T	L	I	M	M	C	J	M
W	T	B	A	L	E	B	M	G	Z	O
A	R	V	L	E	E	Q	T	A	M	H
R	X	O	Z	A	L	L	A	N	M	T
D	C	U	Y	K	C	J	K	X	D	A
S	A	B	R	E	M	N	E	R	L	K
S	H	B	E	U	Z	E	L	I	N	Y

THE WEIRD AND WONDERFUL SIDE OF THE BEAUTIFUL GAME

We've had our fair share of understanding that football is "a funny old game" at Easter Road. Notably in 2014 when, during a pre-season friendly against Dunfermline at Easter Road, Hibs defender Callum Booth launched a mighty clearance. The soaring ball struck a seagull which had been minding its own business swooping around. The bird took a bit of a dive, but rather than risk the referees censure recovered its dignity and flight path.

Who could forget Neil Lennon's "aeroplane" run onto the pitch when Hibernian scored to tie the thrilling final match of the 2017/18 season, against Rangers 5-5 at Easter Road. When Jamie McLaren scored in injury time, the boss couldn't help himself and his iconic aeroplane was swiftly followed by a march up the tunnel as he was red-carded.

But football's funny moments aren't just confined to Hibs, or to Scotland.

Here's a thing you won't often read…

Kick-off in a Highland League match between Fort William and Nairn County in 2019 was delayed by a half hour, with Nairn tweeting "Kick off suspended until 3.30pm due to the ref being delayed with the pitch currently waterlogged and covered in deer faeces."

In 2018, Queen of the South had a selection issue thrown up when 19-year-old goalkeeper Sam Henderson was injured – by a runaway cow! The young goalie, who had been on the bench for the Doonhamers, had suffered a shoulder injury inflicted by the bovine when working on his father's farm.

Back-up Sutton United goalie (no capital 'g' on 'goalie') Wayne Shaw ate a pie during a live, televised 5th round FA Cup tie in season 2016/17. It was later revealed that a bookmaker had offered odds of 8-1 that the 45-year-old keeper would eat a pie on camera. He was subsequently fined and banned by the FA for breaching betting rules.

CLUB HISTORY AND HONOURS

A Few Hibernian Firsts

Hibernian was the first British club to compete in European competition, reaching the semi finals of the European Cup in 1956 Eddie Turnbull became the first British player to score in European competition the same season, scoring in a 4-0 away win against German champions Rot-Weiss Essen.

The first ever women's international football match between Scotland and England took place at Hibernian Park (now the Sunnyside premises of the Hibernian Supporters Association) on May 7th 1881 Hibernian became the first Scottish club to have a sponsors logo on their shirts (Bukta) in 1977, and in 1980 were the first Scottish club to install under soil heating.

Leagues

Scottish Division 1 was the top flight from 1890 – 1975. During that period 4 league titles were achieved, largely due to the renowned team of the Famous Five, during the club's golden period in 1948, 1951 and 1952. An earlier title had been won in 1903. Hibernian have been runners-up on six occasions, in 1897, 1947, 1950, 1953, 1974 and 1975.

The Scottish Cup

The Club has won the Cup on three occasions, in 1887, 1902 and then, of course, on May 21st, 2016, when Rangers were defeated 3-2 at Hampden to end the oldest hoodoo in Scottish football. Runners-up medals have been collected 11 times, illustrating the heartache that was ended in 2016, through teams 1958, 1972, 1979, 2001, 2012, and 2013.

Scottish League Cup

Three Hibernian captains have raised this trophy - Pat Stanton in 1972, Murdo McLeod in 1991 and Rob Jones in 2007, with the club runners-up in 1950, 1969, 1974, 1985, 1993, 2004, 2016.

Minor Honours

The Club has also won the second flight of Scottish league football, now known as the Championship and previously as Division Two, on six occasions – 1894, 1895, 1933, 1981, 1999 and 2017. The Drybrough Cup was won in 1972 and 1973, the Summer Cup in 1941 and 1964, and the Southern League Cup in 1944.

QUIZ ANSWERS

Season Quiz:

1. 3 – the Scottish and League Cup semis for season 2020-21, plus the delayed Scottish Cup semi from the previous season.
2. 4-0 v Hamilton in December
3. Scott Brown, who received a presentation from Hibs skipper David Gray

4. Third
5. Kilmarnock
6. John Hughes

7. Alex Gogic, v Kilmarnock January 2021
8. Scott Allan
9. Dundee Utd
10. Thank You NHS – the first team in the UK to bear the message of thanks to NHS workers for their pandemic heroics

11. St Johnstone
12. Craig Samson
13. St Mirren
14. Jackson Irvine

Player Chat:

1. Matt Macey
2. Ryan Porteous
3. Christian Doidge
4. Melker Hallberg
5. Kyle Magennis
6. Kevin Nisbet
7. Jamie Murphy
8. Joe Newell
9. Lewis Stevenson
10. Kevin Dabrowski

Player Quiz:
1. Arsenal
2. Kevin Nisbet
3. Chris Cadden
4. Alex Gogic
5. Kevin Nisbet, 18 in all competitions
6. Paul McGinn
7. Josh Doig
8. Martin Boyle

Hibernian Riddler Nickname Quiz:
1. Budgie (John Burridge)
2. Sodjer (Alex Cropley)
3. Boyler (Martin Boyle)
4. Porto (Ryan Porteous)
5. The Quiet Man (Pat Stanton)
6. Onion (John Brownlie)
7. Le God (Franck Sauzee)
8. The Little Magician (Russell Latapy)
9. Yogi (John Hughes)
10. Meatball (John McGinn)
11. Sloop (John Blackley)
12. Rocky (Ofir Marciano)
13. Rebel (Eric Stevenson)
14. Crunchie (Kevin McAllister)
15. The Hulk (Tony Higgins)
16. Nijinsky (Arthur Duncan)

Spot the ball:

Wordsearch:

Spot the difference:

Stadium Address:
Easter Road Stadium, 12 Albion Place, Edinburgh, EH7 5QG

Email:
club@hibernianfc.co.uk

Telephone:
0131 661 2159

Social Media
Facebook: Hibernian Football Club Official
Instagram: HibernianFootballClub
Twitter: @HibernianFC
LinkedIn: Hibernian FC
YouTube: Hibernian FC

Ticket Office
Email: tickets@hibernianfc.co.uk

Opening Hours:
Monday to Friday, 10am-5pm
(email and telephone only)
Fridays in person between 10am - 2pm

Clubstore
Email: info@hiberniandirect.co.uk
Telephone: 0131 656 7078

Hospitality:
hospitality@hibernianfc.co.uk